stitute of Leadership
Management

superseries

Influencing
Others at
Work

FIFTH EDITION

Published for the
Institute of Leadership & Management

ELSEVIER

AMSTERDAM • BOSTON • HEIDELBERG • LONDON • NEW YORK • OXFORD
PARIS • SAN DIEGO • SAN FRANCISCO • SINGAPORE • SYDNEY • TOKYO
Pergamon Flexible Learning is an imprint of Elsevier

Pergamon
Flexible
Learning

Pergamon Flexible Learning is an imprint of Elsevier
Linacre House, Jordan Hill, Oxford OX2 8DP, UK
30 Corporate Drive, Suite 400, Burlington, MA 01803, USA

First edition 1986
Second edition 1991
Third edition 1997
Fourth edition 2003
Fifth edition 2007

Editor: David Pardey

Based on material in previous editions of this work

The views expressed in this work are those of the authors and do
not necessarily reflect those of the Institute of Leadership &
Management or of the publisher

British Library Cataloguing in Publication Data
A catalogue record for this book is available from the British Library

Library of Congress Cataloguing in Publication Data
A catalogue record for this book is available from the Library of Congress

ISBN: 978-0-08-046435-0

For information on all Pergamon Flexible Learning publications
visit our website at http://books.elsevier.com

Institute of Leadership & Management
Registered Office
1 Giltspur Street
London
EC1A 9DD
Telephone: 020 7294 2470
www.i-l-m.com
ILM is part of the City & Guilds Group

Typeset by Charon Tec Ltd (A Macmillan Company), Chennai, India
www.charontec.com
Printed and bound in Great Britain

07 08 09 10 11   10 9 8 7 6 5 4 3 2 1

Contents

Contents

Series preface

Whether you are a tutor/trainer or studying management development to further your career, Super Series provides an exciting and flexible resource to help you to achieve your goals. The fifth edition is completely new and up-to-date, and has been structured to perfectly match the Institute of Leadership & Management (ILM)'s new unit-based qualifications for first line managers. It also harmonizes with the 2004 national occupational standards in management and leadership, providing an invaluable resource for S/NVQs at Level 3 in Management.

Super Series is equally valuable for anyone tutoring or studying any management programmes at this level, whether leading to a qualification or not. Individual workbooks also support short programmes, which may be recognized by ILM as Endorsed or Development Awards, or provide the ideal way to undertake CPD activities.

For learners, coping with all the pressures of today's world, Super Series offers you the flexibility to study at your own pace to fit around your professional and other commitments. You don't need a PC or to attend classes at a specific time – choose when and where to study to suit yourself! And you will always have the complete workbook as a quick reference just when you need it.

For tutors/trainers, Super Series provides an invaluable guide to what needs to be covered, and in what depth. It also allows learners who miss occasional sessions to 'catch up' by dipping into the series.

Super Series provides unrivalled support for all those involved in first line management and supervision.

Unit specification

Title:	Influencing others at work		Unit Ref:	M3.31
Level:	3			
Credit value:	1			

Learning outcomes	Assessment criteria	
The learner will	*The learner can (in an organization with which the learner is familiar)*	
1. Understand the value of networking	1.1	Explain the value to the First Line Manager of networking
	1.2	Identify an appropriate network for a First Line Manager and describe methods to establish and maintain effective professional relationships with the identified network
2. Know how to influence/ negotiate with others to achieve objectives	3.1	Explain the general principles of negotiation
	3.2	Explain a relevant technique for influencing others to achieve workplace objectives
	3.3	Describe how to reduce resistance and minimize conflict to achieve a win–win situation in the workplace during negotiations

Workbook introduction

1 ILM Super Series study links

This workbook addresses the issues of *Influencing Others at Work*. Should you wish to extend your study to other Super Series workbooks covering related or different subject areas, you will find a comprehensive list at the back of this book.

2 Links to ILM qualifications

This workbook relates to the learning outcomes of Unit M3.31 Influencing others at work from the ILM Level 3 Award, Certificate and Diploma in First Line Management.

3 Workbook objectives

Winston Churchill was a remarkable leader. All through the Second World War people across the United Kingdom would huddle round their wireless sets listening to his speeches. He seemed to understand how ordinary people were feeling, their fears of invasion, their anxiety about loved ones away fighting the enemy. He was able to use that understanding, that 'empathy', to inspire his fellow citizens to keep fighting with a determination that, in the end, won the War.

Churchill's skills at oratory are legendary. Such phrases as 'We will fight them on the beaches' still live on in people's memories, but where did he acquire the skill to deliver such a powerful message? Most people are surprised to learn that he had a speech impediment, and hated public speaking and shook with fear at the thought of it.

Speaking in public is high on most people's list of things they dread most. The image of all those faces staring at us and waiting for a brilliant display of rhetoric is enough to make us weak at the knees.

But it needn't be like that. By following a few simple rules and, like Churchill, doing a great deal of practice, you can master the skills needed to communicate confidently and with authority.

Session A of this workbook helps you to develop your communication skills so that you will be able to deliver clear and effective briefings to members of your team and others in your work environment.

One of Churchill's many abilities was to 'tune in' to the mood of the nation. He understood intuitively the feelings and emotions of those around him, and knew how to respond to them. This ability to communicate at the subconscious level is the subject of Session B. You will learn how to deduce what people are thinking and feeling from the way they behave, the way they speak and, often, the hidden messages underlying what they say.

However good you are at communicating at the conscious or subconscious level, you can't be sure that you know all you need to know about every subject you are involved in. Session C looks at ways in which you can build a network of people with the experience and knowledge you need to achieve your objectives both in the workplace and outside it.

3.1 Objectives

When you have completed this workbook you will be better able to:

- use your senses to gather information from those around you;
- use the technique of whole body listening to pick up hidden messages;
- explain the value of networking, and create a network to promote both your work objectives and social interests;
- apply the principles of influence and persuasion to achieve objectives.

An effective briefing will often involve the creation and delivery of a visual presentation of your information and so this is also tackled in this workbook.

Session A
Active listening

1 Introduction

Don and Angela were first line managers in a woollen mill. One day all managers in the company were called to a briefing by the CEO. He announced that a major new Icelandic range was about to be introduced which would enable the company to recover its share of the international wool market. The new range would replace certain other product lines that were being discontinued, and he was sure that, in next three months, they would be re-hiring many of their former staff to handle the additional work load.

Walking back to their department after the briefing, Don turned to Angela and said:

'Fantastic. Wait till I tell the rest of the team about this. It should mean loads of overtime at least until Christmas.'

Angela replied:

'Don't you believe it, Don. I reckon we'll be looking for new jobs long before then.'

What had Angela heard that Don hadn't? How had two people listening to the same briefing come away with such different impressions?

Many people use only part of their listening ability. Some, Like Don, only **hear** the 'surface' of what is being said. They don't notice the hidden messages that

1

lie beneath the surface. Others, like Angela, really know how to **listen**, and so are able to:

- glean much more valuable information;
- become aware of the hidden meanings behind what is being said;
- recognize the unconscious signals being given out;
- encourage people to reveal more than they had intended.

In this session we will look at the way we use our senses to gather information from those around us and how, by learning to listen 'actively' and observe people's behaviour, we can identify and interpret the real messages hidden in what they say.

2 The five senses

Activity I

12 mins

Go into the reception area of your organization and stand quietly for a few minutes with your eyes shut. Make a mental note of what you hear, smell and feel. When you have finished, write down your observations below.

_____

_____

_____

_____

_____

You will probably have sensed such things as people moving around, the receptionist talking on the telephone or to visitors, a draught coming through the entrance doors, the smell of the furniture, floor polish and perhaps flowers, security cameras.

All this information is being fed into your brain through your five physical senses:

- sight;
- smell;
- hearing;
- taste;
- touch.

They provide you with a huge amount of detail about what is going on around you.

2.1 Perception

The process through which the brain interprets the information received from the senses is called 'perception'.

If, as a first line manager, you can develop your skills of perception, i.e. improve your ability to take in and interpret all the messages received through your five senses, you will be much better able to:

- pick up the hidden meanings in what people say;
- understand how your team members really feel;
- empathize with their problems;
- improve your communication skills;
- read the non-verbal cues which reveal what people really think.

We use our senses to build an image of what the people around us are like and how they will affect us.

But there can be problems. Our interpretation of the information we take in can be distorted by a number of factors that have nothing to do with the information itself. Two of the most significant factors are:

- the environment in which we are receiving the information (for example, whether it is a bright, warm sitting room or a dark, cold, noisy street);
- our memory of similar experiences, places and people we have known in the past.

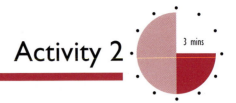

Activity 2

Write down what comes into your mind when you see the words 'Happy New Year'.

_____

_____

_____

The phrase 'Happy New Year' will have triggered in your mind all sorts of sights, sounds and feelings which effect your perception of a happy new year, and which are influenced by your experience of new years in the past.

2.2 Sixth sense

We have another sense, a 'sixth sense', which is independent of our other five senses. Another name for this sense is 'intuition'.

Activity 3

What do we mean by 'intuition'? Write down at least three words which you could use to define it.

_____

_____

_____

_____

If you look up 'intuition' in a thesaurus you will find words such as 'impression', 'premonition', 'hunch', 'feeling', 'anticipation' and 'clue'. The dictionary defines it as 'instinctive knowing without the use of rational processes'.

So we could say that intuition is the sense that enables us to 'feel' what people are like, and therefore what they are likely to do and what they are likely to say.

As with the other senses, there are a number of factors which influence our sixth sense and which may interfere with our ability to perceive other people clearly and non-judgementally. They include our:

■ background, education and personality;
■ experience of similar situations in the past;
■ preconceptions of how things **ought** to be;
■ self interest, i.e. what suits us best;
■ cultural norms, age, gender, class, religion, ethnic origin;
■ mind patterns.

2.3 Mind patterns

As a result of the research into neuro-linguistic programming (NLP) in recent years a great deal has become known about the way in which the brain perceives reality. The way each of us perceives that reality is known as our 'mind pattern'. Information is taken into the brain through certain 'filters' and, by learning to manage the filters, you can develop your sixth sense to help you understand and build a rapport with other people.

You use filters to let some information into your mind and keep other information out. For example, you may look at a situation and mainly notice the positive things about it and ignore the negative – one person might think of a foreign holiday in terms of sunlight, relaxation and adventure (positive), while another person only sees airport delays and tummy bugs (negative). They are both seeing the information (the thought of the holiday) through the same filter (the 'Towards/Away from' filter explained below), but each of them is using it in a different way.

Some common types of filter are as follows.

Filter	Characteristic
Towards/Away from	Towards: when thinking about a future goal (such as a wonderful holiday), you tend to imagine what it would be like to achieve it. Away from: when thinking about the future goal, you tend to think about what might stop you achieving it.
Match/Mismatch	What do you notice about the above shapes? Match: your first thought is that two of the shapes are similar – you always tend to see similarities before differences. Mismatch: your first thought is that one of the shapes is different – you tend to notice differences between things rather than similarities.
Internal/External	Internal: you tend to rely on your own internal feelings to judge whether or not you have done a good job. External: you tend to need external people or events (such as repeat orders) to tell you whether or not you have done a good job.
Past/Present/Future	Past: you like to dwell on the past, and enjoy reminiscing about times gone by. Present: you live for the moment; your attention is on the present. Future: you are constantly planning and thinking about the future.

Activity 4

4 mins

Read the following descriptions and decide which filters each person is using. The first one has been done for you as an example.

I   Eleanor is a great one for living life to the full. She enjoys her job, and knows she is good at it. She plans to be a director by the time she is 30.

Eleanor has 'towards', 'internal' and 'future' filters.

_____

2   Paul loves nothing better than a good argument. He rarely admits that he may be wrong, and can't wait for the day when he will be appointed captain of his local scrabble club.

_____

_____

3   Jan would like to follow in her mother's footsteps and qualify as a librarian. She knows what satisfaction it can bring, but is afraid that she won't be any good at it. The main problem is that she is no good at exams.

_____

_____

The answers to this Activity can be found on page 89.

If the person you are communicating with filters a piece of information in a way which is different from you, then problems of communication are likely to arise.

But once you have recognized the filters that each of you is using, you can choose whether or not to change your filter to match the other person's, so that you are both seeing the situation in the same or complementary ways.

> Brian was discussing a change in work rotas with a member of his team, Sally. He thought that if he swapped one of her shifts with Gus, the result would be a much more efficient way of working. But Sally was reluctant. It had been tried before, she said, and hadn't worked and, anyway, they had used the current system for years with no problems.

Sally was filtering the idea of change through the past. To her the past was best. Understanding this, Brian was able to quote instances in the past when such a change had worked well in other teams, and this helped to overcome Sally's reluctance.

3 The communication process

We use spoken communication to send and receive information and messages. This is rarely, if ever, a one-way process. Generally a sender will send a **message** to someone else, whom we call a receiver, and in return is given **feedback**. The message can be distorted by filters (which we have just considered) and interference (which we will look at later in this session).

The communication process therefore looks like this:
The diagram illustrates that communication is an out-and-back process. A sender sends a communication out to a receiver, who in turn sends one back.

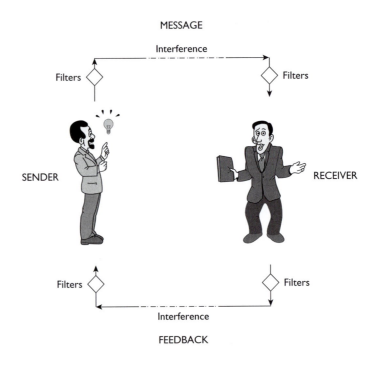

> In an effective communication, both sender and receiver need to send messages, and both need to listen.

This return communication – feedback – tells the original sender whether or not:

- the message has got through;
- action has been or will be taken;
- the purpose has been achieved.

In other words, feedback tells us whether or not the communication process has worked.

3.1 The importance of feedback

David sits in an enclosed office and keeps the door shut. He can't see or hear the other team members, and they can't see or hear him. When he wants to speak to them, he uses a microphone connected to a loudspeaker outside his office.

There is no doubt that everyone can hear him. The question is: how does David know whether anything is happening as a result?

Activity 5   2 mins

Let's imagine that the walls of David's office suddenly vanish, and he makes the same communication face-to-face with his team.

Now how does he know whether anything is happening as a result?

The answer is something that we all experience every day. As David begins to speak:

- the team members first show that they are reacting by paying attention, usually by pausing in their work and turning to look at him;
- they show signs of understanding his message by nodding, making notes or other visual signals;
- they may demonstrate attention by seeking clarification – by asking questions;
- they may signal acceptance of the message by nodding, or saying 'OK', etc.

David will therefore know whether his briefing has been successful by the team members:

- verbally confirming that they have heard and understood;
- demonstrating their understanding in some other way.

3.2 The effect of interference

Research has shown that verbal communication can be very unreliable. It can be affected by blurring, distortion and misinterpretation, and as much as a third can be lost in transmission.

But why do we find it so difficult to listen properly? We're always complaining that other people didn't understand what we meant, or didn't remember what we told them. Yet most of us are just as bad when we listen to others.

On the whole, human beings are rather bad listeners. We fail in three main ways:

The key issue when you are trying to take in information is to think about the sender.

- we don't concentrate hard enough when we listen;
- we don't always check when we don't understand;
- we find it hard to take in and remember more than a small amount of information at a time.

Activity 6 · 15 mins

Listen to the main news bulletin on the radio or television for 10 minutes. Then make a list of all the news items that were mentioned, in the order in which they were presented.

_____

_____

_____

_____

_____

You may have found it surprisingly difficult to do this Activity. Many people are unable to concentrate totally for 10 minutes. It is something you should keep in mind when briefing your team and others at work.

3.3 Creating barriers

We have already learned that the way we take information in can be distorted by the way we **unconsciously** perceive things.

Listeners may also **consciously** erect barriers against incoming communications, for example, when they:

Becoming a better listener will help you spot problems early, defuse conflicts and maintain effective and productive working relationships.

- don't like the message;
- dislike or mistrust the sender;
- are not motivated to listen;
- think they already know the message;
- have a better idea;
- have something better to say;
- pre-judge the content to be irrelevant, uninteresting, too simple or too complex.

This is quite a serious weakness but something can be done about it:

- speakers can learn to 'package' their communications better;
- listeners can learn to listen better.

4 Learning to listen actively

EXTENSION I
How to be Twice as Smart is full of useful tips on how to develop your potential as an individual and as a team leader.

In his book *How to be Twice as Smart*, Scott Witt suggests four basic rules for gathering information that other people miss. These rules are as follows:

- encourage others to talk;
- concentrate on content rather than delivery;
- keep your mind open;
- learn to ignore distractions.

Let's look at each of these in turn.

4.1 Encourage others to talk

You may think that listening is a passive activity – you receive the information being transmitted by the other person and that is the end of it. But this isn't true. Listening is much more dynamic than that.

By learning to listen actively, you can control the direction and flow of the conversation, and the amount of detail that the speaker gives. The secret is to show that you are truly interested.

EXTENSION 2
Written in 1936, *How to Win Friends and Influence People* was one of the first books to introduce popular theories on interpersonal relationships to the general public.

In his celebrated book *How to Win Friends and Influence People*, Dale Carnegie tells of the occasion on which he met an eminent botanist at a dinner party in New York. He spent the evening encouraging his fellow guest to tell him about his research into new plant types and the life cycle of the potato.

At the end of the evening, the botanist delightedly told their host that Carnegie was 'most stimulating' and 'a most interesting conversationalist', even though he had hardly uttered a word.

Carnegie had been an excellent listener. He had used his listening skills to:

■ give the botanist every opportunity to speak;
■ show genuine interest in what he was saying;
■ avoid intruding with his own information, interpretations or concerns.

The result was that the botanist had been made to feel important, interesting and valued, and he, in turn, now saw Carnegie in the same light, even though he had uttered scarcely a word throughout the 'conversation'.

4.2 Concentrate on content rather than delivery

One of the high points in the last few political elections in Europe and the USA has often been a pre-election televised debate between the leaders of the main parties. The candidates usually dread them because they know that **the way** they come across to the voters is far more important than **what** they say.

Politicians and others are trained to use persuasive presentation skills to achieve a goal which may not always be in the best interest of their audience.

Activity 7

2 mins

Think back to the last time you bought something for yourself that you didn't really want. What made you buy it?

_____

_____

Many people are persuaded to buy products because they have been won over by the charm of the salesperson. Indeed, sales trainees are often taught how to sell **themselves** even more than how to sell the benefits of the **product**.

But if you are aware that you are the subject of such persuasion techniques, you can begin to concentrate on the features of the product itself rather than the salesperson's patter.

4.3 Keep your mind open

If you are listening to someone, but are mentally arguing with what they are saying, you could be blocking out information which, in fact, could be useful to you. You might interrupt him, so that he stops talking, or you might even be tempted to think 'he is talking rubbish', and stop listening altogether.

In either case, you are denying yourself the opportunity of hearing something which could be of some use to you if you listen to it with an open mind.

Activity 8

5 mins

Next time you hear someone on television or radio news with whom you usually disagree, instead of mentally 'switching off' listen carefully to what they are saying, and see if you can catch some useful information which you would normally have missed.

4.4 Learn to ignore distractions

Activity 9 · 4 mins

Imagine that you are attending a presentation on a new piece of technology that will soon be introduced in your work area. Because of accommodation problems the presentation is taking place in the staff restaurant. As it happens, a cleaner is sweeping the floor, three people are eating sandwiches at the next table, and the kitchen staff are noisily preparing lunch in the kitchen next door.

What techniques could you use to help you concentrate on what is being said?

_____

_____

_____

You may have suggested moving closer to the speaker, cupping your hands round your ears, or even asking the speaker to speak up. But there are other techniques which will also help you to ignore such distractions. These are:

- taking notes;
- playing mind games;
- using memory techniques.

Taking notes

In order to take notes of what is being said, you need to take the information in, process it in your mind, and then reproduce it in your own words before writing it down. You can't do this without really concentrating.

Playing mind games

Research has shown that, by playing mental games with what is being said, you can become so involved that there is no room left in your mind for the distraction. You could, for instance, try to pick out the longest word in each sentence or, at regular intervals, make a mental summary of what the speaker is saying.

Using memory techniques

The third technique for avoiding distractions is to use word associations to remember key points in the briefing. This is how it works.

Say, for example, that the speaker is talking about the five characteristics of a good learning objective, i.e. it must be:

Specific;
Measurable;
Achievable;
Relevant;
Time bound.

You would do the following.

1 Think of an acronym that represents the key points – in our example it would be the first letters of each characteristic, i.e. SMART.

2 Now use your imagination to create a scene that links 'SMART' with 'learning objectives'. The more ludicrous the scene the better. So you could, perhaps, visualize a small schoolboy with a huge forehead standing in front of a chalk-board which has the word 'SMART' and 'LEARNING OBJECTIVES' written on it in big red letters.

From now on, when you think of 'learning objectives', your mind will immediately associate it with your imagined scene and the word 'SMART'.

This technique will only work if:

■ you fully understand the facts that you want to remember;
■ you have decided that you really want to remember them.

5 Whole body listening

We have already met some of the ideas involved in the study of neuro-linguistic programming (NLP). Another of its theories is that, if you listen to people with your 'whole body', you will not only hear clearly what they are saying, but you will also gain an insight into what they are thinking and feeling.

To listen to someone in this way, you need to give your total attention – your 'whole body' – to what they are saying and how they are saying it.

EXTENSION 3
Sue Knight's book has many helpful hints on how to use NLP to build successful relationships at work.

According to Sue Knight in her excellent introductory book on NLP, *NLP at Work*, the key to whole body listening is to keep your attention external to yourself rather than being involved in your own thoughts. She compares people whose attention is internal with people who are listening with their whole body.

People whose attention is internal	People who are listening with their whole body
They think their own thoughts, make evaluations and judgements. They worry and concentrate on what just happened, what was just said or even what might happen next.	They are in a state of curiosity. Their attention is entirely on the other person.
Their intention is towards themselves.	Their intention is towards the other person.
Their gaze may be de-focused or moving around.	Their gaze is on the other person.
Their posture could be anything.	They match the other person's posture.
Their language is likely to be 'I', 'me' centred.	Their language is 'you' centred and they use the key words and language patterns that match the person with whom they are speaking.

Activity 10

25 mins

Ask a friend, colleague or family member to help you to carry out this Activity.

Find a quiet location where you won't be interrupted.

1 Talk to your friend for five minutes about any topic you choose. Your friend shouldn't make any interruptions during this time. After five minutes ask him or her to summarize what you said, and what your thoughts and feelings were during the talk. Make a note of any significant misinterpretations, omissions or errors in their summary.

2 Repeat the exercise, but this time ask your friend to talk for five minutes on any topic of their choice. Listen using the whole body listening technique. Then repeat back what you have heard and ask them to comment on the accuracy of your account. Make a note of their comments.

You will probably find that listening with your whole body has enabled you to gather much more information and a much clearer insight into the other person's thoughts and feelings.

6 Hidden messages

There is a Chinese proverb which says:

'A man without a smiling face must not open a shop'.

We are all brought up from a very early age to show an acceptable face to the outside world, whatever we may feel inside. But you only have to watch celebrities and people used to being in the public eye to realize that, very often, what they say is not necessarily what they think or feel.

Activity 11

8 mins

During the next few days make a note of examples of people in the news who are probably not saying what they are really thinking or feeling.

Nearly everything we say has at least two meanings:

- the obvious (overt) meaning, which is open and easily observable;
- the hidden (covert) meanings (which can only be observed through developing your skills of perception).

For example, if a friend tells you that he doesn't want a lift home in your car because it is too far out of your way he could actually be thinking that you are a terrible driver.

By learning to look behind the diplomacy to the hidden meanings in people's speech you can gain great advantages in negotiating with your team and with others around you.

6.1 Flag words

According to Witt, there are certain words ('flag' words) that, when used in conversation, are a pretty reliable sign that the speaker does not mean what he or she is saying. The words are as follows:

EXTENSION 1
See *How to be Twice as Smart* by Scott Witt.

- ■ 'of course', 'naturally', 'no doubt' – used when the speaker thinks that something is highly unlikely. For example, 'Naturally we will consider giving you a rise in six months' time';
- ■ 'by the way', 'incidentally' – used when the speaker wants to make something seem less important than it is. For example, 'By the way, there is a railway line just over the garden wall, but we hardly ever hear anything';
- ■ 'I can't because. . .' – used when someone actually **can**. For example, 'I can't set the deadline any later because my boss won't let me'.

6.2 Content Analysis

Content analysis is a technique used by governments and organizations to decode what other governments and organizations really mean, i.e. what their covert meanings are.

By looking at the frequency with which speakers use certain words or mention certain themes, you can discover what is really on their minds. If one of your team often mentions the benefits of working flexi-hours, it is a good bet that, sooner or later, they will ask for a transfer to a team that offers it.

At this point you should be able to understand how, in the case study at the beginning of this session (see page 1), Content analysis enabled Angela to pick up the hidden messages in the CEO's speech. Even though his overt message was that business was looking up, his mention of recovering market share, discontinued product lines and workforce being below strength all indicated that things were in fact far from well. On their own, none of these things should ring alarm bells but, taken together, they could indicate that something was seriously wrong.

 # 7 Non-verbal communication

When talking to other people, we communicate not only with words but with a whole range of gestures, movements and expressions.

In verbal communication, less than half the message is transmitted through what you say. The rest is transmitted in non-verbal ways.

In this section we will look at ways in which you can pick up both overt and covert messages by observing people's body language.

7.1 Common signs and signals

Before human beings discovered how to talk, and long before they discovered how to write, they communicated – like other animals do – by means of a visual language of physical signals and signs.

Two common signals that we still use in the UK today are:

- nodding the head to show agreement;
- giving the 'thumbs up' to show approval.

Activity 12

4 mins

List six or seven other signals that we commonly use to communicate non-verbally.

_____

_____

_____

_____

_____

_____

_____

Suggested answers to this Activity can be found on page 89.

These are large gestures which we use deliberately as an extension of our ordinary language, or in situations where our voices wouldn't be heard, but body language goes much further than this.

7.2 Picking up non-verbal signals

Research has shown that, when communicating, most of us have a natural tendency to make assumptions about the ability of others to 'get the message'. It may simply be because we are lazy, but the danger is that we will overestimate the degree to which they have understood what we are trying to say.

But how can we check that they are keeping up with us?

Activity 13 · 2 mins

Suppose you have to give complicated instructions to someone about whom you know virtually nothing. How can you judge the level of their knowledge and language ability?

_____

_____

_____

With people you have met before, experience should tell you how much they already know. With people you don't know, the simplest way is to ask them. Ask before you start and ask again as you go along – and you should check their understanding frequently if there is any doubt.

You can also use your eyes, because people unconsciously send out signals and signs all the time. The way they behave will give you a clue as to what is happening in their minds.

Whether you are speaking to one person or a group, the unconscious body language of your listeners gives you enormously valuable feedback. You will be able to tell whether or not you are holding their attention, and whether or not you are getting your messages across.

Activity 14

2 mins

Suppose you are telling work-experience trainees about the work your section does. What visual signs would show that you are not holding their attention?

_____

_____

_____

> Humans are usually much better at recognizing body language than at listening to speech – it's a skill our species acquired much, much earlier.

There are many signs that you should recognize. We have all sent similar signals in our time.

Signs of boredom:
- saying 'uh huh', 'yes', or 'right' before you have finished a sentence;
- looking around.

Meaning: they want you to get on with it.

Signs of difficulty keeping up:
- puzzled expression (furrowed brow, screwed-up eyes, etc.);
- scratched heads.

Meaning: they are still trying, but they have trouble keeping up with you.

Signs of failing concentration:
- yawning, looking at their watches, looking around;
- doodling, fidgeting, picking, scratching, shuffling, passing notes.

Meaning: you are losing them fast – they have stopped trying to concentrate.

EXTENSION 4
A helpful book on the subject of body language is *Body Talk: the skills of positive image* by Judi James.

Signs of having given up:
- glazed expressions;
- falling asleep.

Meaning: you've lost them – and you probably won't be able to get them back.

7.3 Responding to conflicting messages

Body language sends messages. When these are consistent with the verbal messages we're trying to communicate there is no problem – the body language reinforces the verbal message.

But when the body language is telling a different story from the verbal message the credibility of the message is weakened. The simplest example of this is when someone tries to make a genuine and sincere statement but is unable make eye contact with the audience.

We use a wide range of facial expressions and body movements that reveal our feelings and our reactions to other people. Often we use these signs without consciously intending to, and often they don't reflect what we are saying.

So how should you react if somebody's body language sends a message which is different from their speech?

We all learn to recognize these signs. We can tell by people's behaviour whether they are excited, bored, tired, mystified, irritated, friendly, hostile, nervous or angry.

Even if you are talking to someone on the telephone, where you can't see each other's body language, you can still hear subtle hesitations and changes in tone which reveal the other person's true feelings.

If you recognize such signs, you have to decide whether you are going to believe:

- their words, or
- their body language.

> Frank was briefing some colleagues on his section's re-organization plans. One or two of them looked interested, nodded from time to time and took notes. However, Frank noticed a couple of others who seemed to spend most of the time doodling, gazing at the posters on the office wall and fiddling with their fingernails.
>
> When he'd finished, Frank looked all round the group and asked 'Does anyone have any questions?' One of the people who had been taking notes asked a question, but neither of the 'doodlers' did. Frank made a final attempt to check: 'Is everyone happy?' All those present either nodded agreement or murmured 'Yes'. But sure enough, it later turned out that the doodlers hadn't grasped the main point of the briefing at all. A couple of weeks later Frank had to brief them all over again.

Activity 15

2 mins

In this case study Frank was right about what the doodlers' body language was telling him. What could he have done in the circumstances?

_____

_____

_____

If Frank had been a school teacher, he would probably have put the doodlers on the spot by asking them some searching questions. However, you just can't do that with colleagues.

The alternative would be to make an extra effort to engage their interest, perhaps by:

- making more eye contact with them than with the others present;
- making references to how their particular departments or functions might be affected by his plans;
- inviting them to contribute to the discussion.

In any situation where a person's body language and words conflict, your best approach is to try to break down any barriers between you and build a good rapport.

We will look at rapport in Session B.

Self-assessment 1

15 mins

1   We use our _____ to build an image of what the people around us are like and how they will effect us.

2   What are our five physical senses?

_____

_____

3   The communication process consists of a sender sending a _____ to a receiver, and in return receiving _____.

4   Why is feedback so important in the communication process?

    _____

    _____

5   Suggest three techniques which will help you to ignore distractions when someone is speaking.

    _____

    _____

    _____

6   What is the secret of active listening?

    _____

    _____

    _____

7   The following list contains descriptions of (1) people whose attention is internal and (2) people who listen with their whole body. Tick the boxes to indicate which is which.

Type of listener	Their attention is internal	They are listening with their whole body
They think their own thoughts, make evaluations and judgements. They worry and concentrate on what just happened, what was just said or even what might happen next.		
Their gaze is on the other person.		
They are in a state of curiosity. Their attention is entirely on the other person.		
Their language is likely to be 'I', 'me' centred.		

8   Suggest two ways in which you can judge the level of knowledge and language ability of someone about whom you know virtually nothing.

_____

_____

9   How might a speaker's body language:

a reduce the speaker's credibility?

_____

b weaken the speaker's message?

_____

Answers to these questions can be found on pages 87–8.

8 Summary

- Human beings are bad listeners because:

  - we don't concentrate hard enough when we listen;
  - we don't always check when we don't understand;
  - we find it hard to take in and remember more than a small amount of information at a time;
  - we erect barriers against people and things that we misjudge, misunderstand or simply don't want to hear.

- Good listeners are able to:

  - glean much more valuable information;
  - become aware of the hidden meanings behind what is being said;
  - recognize the unconscious signals being given out;
  - encourage people to reveal more than they had intended.

- We have five physical senses, sight, smell, hearing, taste and touch.

- The sixth sense is intuition.

- We use filters to let certain information into our minds and keep other information out.

- Feedback tells us whether or not the communication process has been successful.

- Up to 30% of verbal communication can be lost in transmission.

- We can gather more information by:

  - encouraging others to talk;
  - concentrating on content rather than delivery;
  - keeping our minds open;
  - learning to ignore distractions.

- Whole body listening involves keeping our attention focused outside ourselves.

- In verbal communication, less than half the message is transmitted through what we say. The rest is transmitted in non-verbal ways.

- In any situation where a person's body language and words conflict, the best approach is to try to break down barriers and build a good rapport.

Session B
Building a network

1 Introduction

Consider Robert...

Robert was an only child. When he was a boy, most Sunday afternoons had been spent on railway platforms, sharing his father's passion for train spotting. At school he had worked hard, preferring to stay behind in the computer room when his classmates played five-a-side football in the playground. He did well in his exams, and won a place to study computer science at university. He made few friends during his student years; he saw no point in spending money in pubs, and believed that the most important thing in life was to justify his parents' belief in him by getting a good degree. This he did.

On graduating, Robert got a job as an IT support technician in an international company not far from his home. His parents were delighted as this meant that he could move back into his old bedroom.

A year later the company hit hard times and Robert was made redundant. There were no jobs around for support technicians with his specialized knowledge and skills, and Robert had no idea what else he could do. The future looked bleak.

Ziggy, on the other hand, had always loved people around her. Her first memory was playing Mary in the school nativity play. She had adored Brownies, learned to ice skate with a crowd of friends, and had been head of nearly every sports team in her school. When she did her Duke of Edinburgh Award, she became deeply involved in supporting underprivileged families in her area and raising money for them. Everyone missed her when she went off to college to do media studies.

College life was fast and furious. Ziggy became a leading light of the drama, square dance and mountaineering clubs, and helped organize numerous social events, culminating in the graduation ball at the end of her final year. When she got a job on one of the national newspapers, no one was a bit surprised.

But, like Robert, Ziggy was made redundant. The paper was taken over and her job was no longer needed. As soon as she heard, Ziggy began firing off emails to everyone she could think of, and within two weeks an old university friend had put her in touch with an international charity which, impressed with her history of social work, hired her to join their international marketing team.

Activity 16

3 mins

What did Ziggy have going for her in her working life that Robert didn't?

_____

_____

Ziggy was very much a 'people' person. She liked nearly everyone she met, understood how to build relationships, and knew how to use those relationships to further her job prospects. In contrast Robert was thoroughly introvert. He looked to things rather than people for his emotional support, and when he was in trouble he didn't have the contacts or social skills to help him get back on his feet.

This session looks at why Ziggy was so much more successful than Robert in relating to people. You will learn how her skill at networking can be developed and maintained in the workplace, and how everyone – you, your team and the organization – can benefit from close-knit, effective networking relationships.

2 What is networking?

2.1 A definition

Networking can be defined as:

'the creation and use of personal contacts for one's own benefit or for the benefit of a group'.

In other words, a network is a set of contacts you develop to promote your career or some other interest.

Networking can be used in any context: at work, in your social life or any other situation. The point is that you are using your contacts with other people to help yourself and them to become more successful.

Ziggy had built up a large network of friends and contacts during her time at school and university, and she was able to use these to further her career when the job market got tough.

2.2 How does a network differ from any other social group?

You are probably already a member of one or more groups of friends or acquaintances who spend time together.

Activity 17

8 mins

Think about the contacts you have (1) at work and (2) socially with whom you have a friendly relationship. Write some of their names below.

Work contacts

_____

_____

_____

_____

_____

_____

Social contacts

_____

_____

_____

_____

_____

_____

You will probably be surprised at how many names you wrote down of people with whom you have some kind of relationship.

A network is different from a group of friends because its sole purpose is to develop a means of interaction which will benefit either you alone or all its members generally. It provides a reservoir of people who have specialist knowledge and contacts that will help you to achieve your chosen objectives.

So it is a much more structured organism than a group of friends and colleagues.

Activity 18

4 mins

Look at the names that you wrote down in the last Activity. Now carry out the same exercise again, but this time limit the names to those people whose knowledge you can use to develop some enterprise or interest you have.

Work contacts

_____

_____

_____

_____

Social contacts

_____

_____

_____

_____

You should now be able to appreciate the difference between a group of friends or colleagues and a network; the former is not necessarily useful to you in achieving your objectives whereas the latter is.

 # 3 What's good about networking?

EXTENSION 1
In his book _How to be Twice as Smart_ Scott Witt describes the benefits of networking.

Networking lets you:

■ tap into the knowledge and experience of other people, without having to learn or experience those things yourself;

■ access the latest information as and when you need it;

■ help other people by offering your own knowledge and experience;

■ become an expert in areas which may not be covered adequately in reference materials;

■ understand a topic from the point of view of people who have practical experience of it, not just the theory;

■ build loyalty and rapport with a group of people who can help each other to achieve their individual aims.

4 Types of network

Networks can be classified in various ways. We will look at two types of classification.

■ internal networks/external networks;

■ knowledge networks/self-interest groups.

4.1 Internal and external networks

Networks relating to your work can be either internal to the organization or external.

Internal networks

Your internal network is likely to consist of colleagues in your own department and in other areas of your organization.

By building links with such people you can obtain information that enables you to:

> If you find out what opposition you are likely to meet before it happens, you can take preventative action.

■ build a good team;

■ give and receive support from other team leaders;

■ learn new skills;

■ identify areas for development;

■ access knowledge and experience held by specialists in other work areas;

■ promote changes which you would like to introduce in your work area;

■ lobby the people whose support you need to achieve your objectives;

■ find out about potential opposition to your plans.

Internal networks are built naturally through your everyday working activities, but if they are to be really effective you have to spend time developing and nurturing them.

You could, for instance:

- establish regular email correspondence with someone in another section who might have information or contacts that could help you in the future;
- join committees relating to your work, union or a company social club;
- become a member of a company sports team.

Every contact made through these actions could prove helpful to you in achieving your personal or work objectives at some time in the future.

External networks

External networks are those you develop with people outside your organization, such as former colleagues or people working for other companies in the same industry. Networks outside the organization can be helpful in many ways:

- if your job is threatened, external contacts in the same line of business might know of other vacancies elsewhere;
- talking to other people can help you to gain information, identify training courses, find useful websites, and so on, all of which could help you develop your career.

Strategies for developing external networks include:

- joining special interest clubs which have relevance to your work (such as the student organizations which exist under the umbrella of some professions);
- using Internet chat rooms relating to particular subject areas;
- developing social links with people from other organizations in your industry.

You can also use external networks to help you in the social side of your life, for instance to:

- make new friends when you move to a new neighbourhood;
- find out the best schools, doctors, dentists, shops;
- locate reliable experts such as plumbers and electricians;
- find out about local organizations such as sports clubs, yoga classes or pub music nights.

4.2 Knowledge networks and mutual interest networks

Another way of classifying networks is to divide them into:

- those that you use specifically to promote your own interests, for example, to develop your career or gain a new skill (known as knowledge networks);
- those whose aim is to benefit all members equally (mutual interest networks).

Knowledge networks

No one can know everything they need to know all the time – for one thing it would soon be out of date. A much more efficient solution is to be able to contact the person who **does** have the latest information, at the time when you need it.

A knowledge network is a ready-reference list of people who are willing and able to give you the information you need when you need it. By creating a knowledge network you can:

- find out the best way to develop your career;
- avoid making mistakes;
- obtain all the information you need to make major decisions;
- build up background data on a situation before you get involved in it.

Steve wanted to buy a new home computer. He already used computers for simple spreadsheet tasks at work, but didn't really understand all the terminology. The magazine adverts looked impressive, but he really had no idea of the best specification for his particular needs: helping his daughter with her homework and working through his home study course on computing. What Steve needed was a knowledge network.

He needed to find people who could tell him about different computer specifications, the advantages and disadvantages of each, and what the best specification would be for him. Any computer shop would have a vested interest in the advice it gave him; he would be much wiser to talk to an experienced colleague or members of the local computer club.

The important thing about knowledge networks is that you should never include anyone who is involved financially in that particular subject area or interest. Only ask for information or advice from people who have nothing to lose by giving it to you. So, for instance, you should never ask:

- an accountant for free advice on your tax return;
- a surveyor to look at your house subsidence as a favour;
- a solicitor to comment on the advice you have received from another law firm.

But you **could** ask any of them for advice on anything else about which they have expert knowledge – so long as it isn't something for which they usually charge.

You might well ask why such people should be prepared to give you information in the first place. What are they going to get out of it?

Well, we have already seen in Session B that people like to be made to feel valued and important – and most people are naturally helpful anyway. So long as they don't feel that they are being exploited, the vast majority of people are only too keen to offer help and advice on their pet subject if they are asked in the right way.

Mutual interest networks

Certain types of knowledge are best learned by joining a group of people who all share their knowledge with each other. Examples include computer groups, share investment groups and groups which form to develop a particular hobby, such as antiques or travel.

Mutual interest networks (MINs) are different from clubs because there is no formal structure – no official membership, no secretary and no committee. They are just a group of people who enjoy sharing their knowledge and enthusiasm for a particular topic. Every member of the network benefits because every member shares information and supports the others.

Activity 19

3 mins

Think about your own interests, both inside your organization and outside. Are there any areas in which you would find it useful to form a MIN?

_____

_____

5 Creating a network

Victoria had worked at the bank for five years. She had passed all her banking exams with flying colours but had hit a 'glass ceiling' – no matter how hard she tried, she just couldn't get promotion within her section of the bank.

Then she read a self-help book on 'How to network effectively', and decided to try out its theories. We will follow her progress during the rest of this section.

Victoria's self-help book explained that developing a network involves the following steps:

1 decide **why** you want to network;

2 decide on a strategy;

3 carry out research;

4 develop the network.

5.1 Decide why you want to network

EXTENSION 5
See *Networking for Success* by Carol Harris for more advice on developing a network.

There are any number of reasons why you might need to obtain knowledge through networking. You might, for example, want to:

■ learn more about a new piece of technology you would like to introduce at work;

■ research the potential for a career move;

■ develop your interest in a particular hobby.

In Victoria's case the purpose was clear: she wanted to develop a network that would help her to advance her career in banking.

Activity 20 · 5 mins

Choose a project to do with either your work or leisure activities in which obtaining expert knowledge from other people could be useful e.g. you might ask a professional caterer about how much food you should serve at a buffet for 180 people. Briefly describe the project and the knowledge you would like to obtain.

_____

_____

_____

5.2 Decide on a strategy

SWOT analysis is usually used in an organizational context. However, it can also be used to assess individuals.

You need to think about the strategy you will use to get the knowledge. It is useful to start with a SWOT analysis which involves analysing your:

- **S**trengths;
- **W**eaknesses;
- **O**pportunities;
- **T**hreats.

You might find that, in developing a network:

- strengths could include the people you know already or any particular ally you already have whom you might call on for help;
- weaknesses could include such things as lack of time or poor communication skills;
- opportunities could include clubs you might join or having access to the Internet;
- threats could include other people resenting your networking activities or opposing the reason for your networking (such as getting a better job).

As far as Victoria was concerned she felt that her main strengths were her friendly personality and the fact that she already worked in a bank. Her main weakness was that being a woman made it more difficult to get promotion in the bank. Her opportunities included the fact that there were other women in the bank who could help her, and she knew that one of the few female senior managers played for the bank's badminton team. Victoria was very good at badminton. Her only threat was that she didn't get on with her immediate manager, so might get some opposition from him.

Activity 21   10 mins

Think about the strengths, weaknesses, opportunities and threats relating to your own project. Make a list of them.

Strengths

_____

_____

Weaknesses

_____

_____

Opportunities

_____

_____

Threats

_____

_____

You may have had a number of ideas. The list will probably grow as you get further into your planning.

Once you have done a SWOT analysis, you can develop a detailed strategy for building your network.

You might, for example, decide that one of your strengths is access to a number of clubs or societies where you can find helpful people, while a weakness is that you are not very good at using your interpersonal skills. So part of your strategy might be to do an open learning course on rapport building. You will learn more about building rapport later in this section.

Other strategies might include:

- making lists of everyone you know already who might be useful to you;
- getting your line manager to support you;
- joining appropriate clubs;
- getting access to the Internet;
- watching what other people around you do to build effective networks;
- finding ways to incorporate your networking activities into your everyday life.

Victoria decided that her main strategies would be to:

- join the bank's badminton team;
- develop a network of the women in her bank and in other banks in the town.

By taking these steps she would gain:

- advance information of any vacancies that cropped up in any local bank;
- a way of getting to know the female senior manager in her own bank;
- information on how other women had dealt with a glass ceiling in the past.

Activity 22 · 10 mins

Make a list of the strategies you will use to develop your network.

_____

_____

_____

_____

5.3 Carry out research

In the last step we saw how, in deciding on a strategy, you should make a list of all those contacts you have already who have knowledge that could be useful to you. (This was the 'strengths' part of the SWOT analysis.) The list might be quite short, but it is just the start.

Each person on it will be able to put you in touch with other people who also have useful knowledge, and in the research phase you should follow up those leads by contacting the people concerned.

The research stage also involves identifying the clubs, social groups, computer chat rooms and other groupings where you might meet the people who can help you. You could do this by:

- viewing appropriate websites;
- looking at trade magazines;
- consulting lists of clubs, societies and trade associations in the local library;
- asking company switchboards for contact details of appropriate members of staff in your own and other organizations;
- checking courses offered by the local further education college;
- contacting relevant professional bodies.

Victoria decided that a good place to start her research would be her local association of the Institute of Financial Services (ifs). She visited the ifs website and discovered:

- the contact details of her local ifs association and a programme of their meetings;
- an annual series of Financial Innovations Awards, one of whose categories was for the best customer relationship management strategy;
- an annual Awards dinner where she would be able to meet useful people;

- a careers development section containing a course aimed at a BSc (Hons) in Financial Services and Associateship;
- a career development service;
- a student learning support (SLS) team.

She decided to find out more about all of these.

Activity 23

Make your own list of contacts and social groups that could be useful to you in your own networking project.

_____

_____

_____

_____

5.4 Develop your network

You have chosen the people to contact, clubs to join and projects to get involved in – all that's left now is to actually start networking.

You don't have to be brazen-faced by asking your contacts directly for the information you want. There is a huge amount that you can glean from a casual conversation which has been steered round to the general topic area.

But what do you do if you have been given the name of someone you have never met before? How can you approach them?

There are three particularly useful techniques:

- mention the name of the person who referred you – for example: 'Anne Davies suggested that you might be able to advise me on ...';
- make the person feel important – for example, 'I have been told that you know everything there is to know about ...';
- make a straightforward appeal for help – for example, 'I would be really grateful if you would tell me how to ...'.

But remember, never ask for free information from an expert whose business involves providing it for a fee.

6 Building rapport

6.1 We all need to relate

Your success at networking will depend on your ability to build effective relationships.

Activity 24 · 35 mins

Next time you are in a social environment such as the staff restaurant, the pub, at home with the family, or somewhere else where you normally meet people socially, try an experiment.

For the first 15 minutes avoid communicating with anyone – no talking, no smiling, no eye contact. During the next 15 minutes look happy, chat with people you meet, crack a joke or two (if you are good at it), and show real interest in everything that is going on around you.

Look at the words below and underline all those words which you think would reflect your feelings at the end if the first 15 minutes; then circle all the words which would reflect your feelings at the end of the second 15 minutes.

happy	shy	embarrassed	self-aware
depressed	optimistic	bored	warm
frustrated	anxious	kind	confident
respected	enthusiastic	ill at ease	tired
successful	disliked	inferior	excluded
funny	sociable	depressed	stimulating
liked	nervous	boring	resentful

The odds are that you underlined most of the negative words to describe the first 15 minutes, and positive ones for the second period when you were chatting to people and communicating generally.

Communication is essential if we are to feel comfortable in the society of other people. And networking is all about communicating well.

Effective communication is based on rapport, i.e. the ability to see the other person's point of view. If you have rapport with someone you are 'on the same wavelength' – even though you don't necessarily share the same opinions. You feel easy in their company, conversation is relaxed and silences are not awkward. You often intuitively know what the other person is thinking, and can understand and empathize with their feelings.

People who share rapport show it in many physical ways. They:

- mirror each other's actions and posture;
- laugh at the same time;
- move in the same rhythm;
- look in the same direction.

They will often do this quite unconsciously, and may often be able to divine each other's thoughts and feelings.

Activity 25

10 mins

Observe the people you are working with during the next couple of days. Do any of them show signs of rapport? If so, what are those signs?

_____

_____

_____

Most of the indicators of rapport consist of matching **physical** behaviour – posture, movement, voice tones and so on. But the rapport between two people will be even stronger if they also share common **values** (such as honesty, truthfulness, loyalty, commitment) and **beliefs** (for example, that everyone is of value or that there is no such thing as failure).

6.2 How to build rapport

If you can build a rapport with someone, you are more likely to be able to network with them than with those you can't.

So how do you build rapport with someone if it doesn't exist naturally between you?

The key is to match their behaviour by:

- matching the way they stand and the way they hold their body;
- holding your arms, hands and fingers in the same way;

- copying the way they hold their head and shoulders;
- looking in the same direction as they do;
- following their gaze;
- breathing at the same rate;
- breathing from the same part of the body (lungs, abdomen, stomach);
- walking to the same rhythm;
- speaking at the same pitch, volume and pace;
- using the same kinds of words and terminology.

You can also use the lessons we learned about mind patterns in Session A to complement the filters they use in processing information. For example, note whether their filters are towards or away from, past, present or future, match or mismatch, internal or external. Then adopt an approach that complements them.

Activity 26 · 10 mins

During the next few days practise your skills of matching with people you meet. Make a note of their reactions. Does conversation flow more easily? Is the atmosphere more relaxed? Have you been successful in building a rapport with them?

6.3 Some final tips

This session has looked at the steps involved in developing a network from scratch. But the basic principles of networking can be applied at every point in your life, both at work and at home.

Here are a few final tips for you to practise until they become second nature to you:

- remember people's names, and use them frequently when talking to them;
- never leave a meeting or other gathering wishing you had spoken to someone;
- find out about the people you are going to contact; know what their interests and priorities are;
- when you meet new contacts for the first time, don't try to pick their brains there and then; get in touch with them later;
- dress smartly so that people notice and remember you;
- always have your contact details with you – and a pen and paper to write down other people's details;

- always keep your promises. If you have said you will do something, do it;
- always send a thank you note after a party;
- form a bond with someone by asking them to do you a favour;
- whenever possible, give people something – even if it is just some notes or a useful telephone number;
- smile.

Self-assessment 2

15 mins

1 Networking can be defined as the creation and use of personal contacts for one's own _____ or for the _____ of a group.

2 What is the difference between a network and a social group?

_____

_____

3 What are the two ways in which networks can be classified?

_____

_____

4 Suggest three ways in which you could develop an internal network.

_____

_____

_____

5 What kind of network is designed specifically to benefit all members equally?

_____

6 Who should you never ask for advice when you are networking?

_____

7 What does SWOT stand for?

_____

8 Can you have rapport with someone if you don't share their opinions?

_____

Answers to these questions can be found on page 88.

7 Summary

- Networking is the creation and use of personal contacts for one's own benefit or for the benefit of a group.

- Networking can be used in any context.

- A network is different from a group of friends because its sole purpose is to develop a means of interaction which will benefit its members.

- Networking lets every member of the network:

  - tap into the knowledge and experience of other people without having to learn or experience those things themselves;
  - access the latest information as and when they need it;
  - help other people by offering their own knowledge and experience;
  - become an expert in areas which may not be covered adequately in reference materials;
  - understand a topic from the point of view of people who have practical experience of it, not just the theory;
  - build loyalty and rapport with a group of people who can help each other to achieve their individual aims.

- Two classifications of 'networking' are:

  - internal networks/external networks;
  - knowledge networks/mutual interest networks.

- You should only ask for information or advice from people who have nothing to lose by giving it to you.

- To develop a network you must:

  - decide why you want to network;
  - decide on a strategy;
  - carry out research;
  - develop the network.

- One of your first strategies is to make a list of all those contacts you have already who have knowledge that could be useful to you.

- Your success at networking will depend on your ability to build effective relationships.

- Having rapport means that you are on the same wavelength as someone – even if you don't share their opinions.

Session C
How to get the result you want

 1 Introduction

As a first line manager you have a number of means at your disposal to get people to do what you want. Sometimes they will respond just as you intended, sometimes not. Sometimes it will involve a lot of effort on your part, sometimes you may even have to compromise. Your success will largely depend on the skills you will learn in this session.

We will consider four ways of getting other people to do what you want.

- Instructing – where you have sufficient power and authority to **tell** someone what to do.
- Influencing – where you bring the whole context of the situation to bear on the other person, including the quality of your past and current working relationship, his or her wants, needs and fears.
- Persuading – where you use all your verbal and non-verbal skills to get the other person to agree.
- Negotiating – where you have the same bargaining power as the other person, and both of you have to compromise in order to get something of what each of you wants.

2 Instructing

As a first line manager you have the power to issue instructions to your workforce. There are a number of ways of getting the message across, some of them more effective than others. Three of these ways are:

- giving orders;
- making a request;
- pleading.

2.1 Orders

We give an order when:

- it's an emergency – where timing is critical;
- an immediate response is needed;
- the people on the receiving end know exactly how to respond.

An example of an order might be:

'Take aim. Fire!'

Orders are right for such jobs as the armed services, police or fire services because there's no time for requests or explanations – an immediate response is needed. Because of the urgency, an order has to be short and to the point. It must also be precise. The normal courtesies of 'please' and 'thank you' are neglected and yet, in circumstances where giving an order is warranted, this is quite acceptable. It is also acceptable in a situation where one person has specialist knowledge and is training someone else how to do something (for example, 'Now, double-click the mouse on the file name, then …').

Most of the time, however, orders aren't a suitable way of getting things done. In most circumstances, people will respond more positively if they are involved in the decision making and understand the reason why something needs to be done.

2.2 Requests

Usually people will respond better if they are **asked** to do something rather than if they are **told** to do it.

This doesn't undermine your power as a manager. A request can easily make clear what you want done, when, why, how and by whom. Giving your instructions in the form of requests doesn't mean that you lose any of your control over the job.

Asking rather than telling makes the team feel that you see them as people with something to offer to the job rather than just cogs in a wheel.

Activity 27 · 3 mins

Here are two very different ways of giving the same instruction. Which do you think is better, and why?

a 'Fred, you're on the gate from 10.30. Hand over to Mr Khan at mid-day.'

b 'I'd like you to go on the gate this morning, Fred. Do 10.30 to mid-day and then hand over to Mr Khan, would you? … Thanks.'

_____

_____

_____

_____

_____

The obvious difference between the two versions is that the first one is an order, the second is a request because it features:

- a question rather than a statement;
- a more personal kind of language ('I'd like you to …');
- a politer turn of phrase;
- a pause, during which the speaker checks Fred's understanding and agreement.

That's all a request need be – a matter of saying 'I'd like you to …' or 'Would you …', or 'Would you mind …' rather than just 'Do this'. But it lets people know that you value them as well as the job. And saying 'Thank you' reminds everyone that you are all human beings who respond best when treated with courtesy.

2.3 Pleading

Sometimes, when you are tired or under pressure, you may feel that the best way to get something done is to plead with the person concerned.

Activity 28 ·   3 mins

A team leader makes the following plea to the computer operator.

'Look, I know that you've been busy, but this job is really urgent. Customer services will be furious if the figures aren't ready by tomorrow morning. So, for my sake, please try and speed it up.'

What do you think about this as a way of getting people to do something for you? What effect would it have on the relationship between you and them?

_____

_____

_____

_____

Well, we have all probably tried to give an instruction in this kind of way at some point, and it may even have worked. But it's a bad idea to try to lead people on the basis of their sympathy or liking for you because:

- by pleading you run the risk that it may reduce your personal power;
- it may appear that you are handing over both control and authority to that person;
- asking someone to carry out a task as a personal favour could place professional working relationships at risk;
- if you ask for favours, sooner or later you will be obliged to return them.

You may be able to use the power of your position to get someone to do something, but it doesn't help you to control **how** they do it. And if you had no power over them, they may not do it at all. In these situations you need to use your personal power to come to an agreement with them. To do this you need to acquire the skills of influencing and persuading.

3 Influencing

By 'influencing' we mean trying to affect someone's behaviour by changing their thoughts, beliefs or attitudes.

Activity 29 · 3 mins

Write down four factors that made you apply for, and then accept, your current job.

_____

_____

_____

_____

You might have mentioned the reputation of the organization, type of work, location of the job, salary, career prospects, opportunities to learn a new skill, and so on. They could all be factors that play a part in influencing your decision to take the job.

You can use influencing factors to great effect in the workplace when you are negotiating with other people. (You will learn more about the specific techniques involved in the negotiating process on page 65.)

By learning about influencing factors you can:

■ create a situation in which your skills of persuasion and negotiation will be most effective;
■ recognize the factors that might influence **you** in a negotiating situation.

The main factors that influence us are as follows:

■ personal relationships;
■ position power;
■ formality;
■ knowledge and expertise;
■ gender, race and age;
■ reputation;

- expectations about outcomes;
- pressure of work and deadlines;
- location.

We will look at each of these in turn.

3.1 Personal relationships

EXTENSION 6
You can learn more about influencing factors in *Negotiating Persuading and Influencing* by Alan Fowler.

Your relationship with the person you are dealing with can have a significant influence on your communication tactics. It can work in the following two ways.

- If relations have been friendly in the past, both of you will begin with the assumption that this will continue, and will make an effort for it do so. If relations have been antagonistic, you will be half expecting the same again, and your words and body language are likely to reflect this.
- If you anticipate that this will be one of a long series of dealings in the future, you will be at pains to keep the relationship friendly, whatever your inner feelings may be.

Personal relationships are particularly important in a close-knit environment such as a team. Whether people like or dislike each other can have a major influence on the team's cohesion, and it can be difficult to work objectively with someone with whom you have a personal problem.

3.2 Position power

Everyone in an organization has the power to influence others. The higher up the organization they are, the more power and influence they have. This, as you saw in Session A, is known as 'position power'.

However, while some people enjoy influence because of their position in the management hierarchy, others have it because they have a particular type of job in the organization.

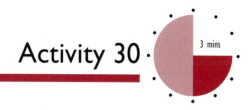

Activity 30

3 mins

Who else at work has influence over you besides the people who are in a higher managerial position than you?

_____

_____

_____

Your suggestions might include the following.

- Security staff: if a security guard insists on searching your bag as you enter the building, you probably won't argue about it.
- The human resource department: if the HR officer tells you that recruitment must be done in a certain way according to company policy, you would probably accept this.
- Experts in IT and other specialists.

If you look at your list, you will see that there two groups.

- People who hold a special position (such as security staff and inspectors).
- People who have special expertise (such as IT experts).

Both groups have the power through their position or expertise to influence the minds and actions of others in the organization.

As far as dealing with other managers in the hierarchy is concerned, there are several strategies at your disposal. Some will be particularly effective when your position power is high. Others will depend more on using personal power.

The strategies include:

- assertiveness – most frequently used when position power is high but success will be difficult to achieve;
- friendliness – often used when both position power and expectations of success are low;
- reason – used frequently when position power and expectations of success are high;
- bargaining;
- referral to a higher authority;
- sanctions or disciplinary action.

One more important point – organizational 'politics' can come into play when you are dealing with a relatively junior colleague who has close connections with senior management. Although this should make no difference to the way you behave, you may well feel that you must be careful of what you say or do.

3.3 Formality

Some people can be overawed if they have to take part in formal communications (such as trades union negotiations). The process is usually more structured than in informal situations, and more people may be involved, but the basic skills are just the same as when you are dealing with a colleague in the workplace. So don't let formal conditions influence your approach.

3.4 Knowledge and expertise

Any expert knowledge you have in the subject under discussion will give you a greater sense of confidence, and this will show in your body language and tone of voice. Expert knowledge is particularly valuable if you are suffering under the negative influences of weak position power or poor personal relationships.

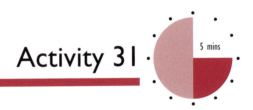

Activity 31 · 5 mins

Think of a recent situation where you have had to take part in discussions on a topic in which you are a real expert. Then compare it with a time when you had to do the same involving a topic you knew little about. How did you feel in each situation? Could you have prepared yourself better for the second situation? If so, how?

Situation 1

_____

_____

_____

Situation 2

_____

_____

_____

You would probably have done better in the second situation if you had done some research first, and you would certainly have found the experience more satisfying.

3.5 Gender, race and age

The influence of gender, race and age on negotiations can be subtle, but is very common, none the less. It can affect both sides, causing one person to feel dominant and the other to feel threatened, with the result that the former may become more aggressive and the latter submissive.

Such discrimination can be difficult to counter as it is often not overtly stated, but shows itself more in a general attitude of superiority. If you come across this type of influence, either in yourself or others, you need to recognize it for what it is and make a conscious effort to eliminate it from your working environment. You can learn more about handling discrimination in _Managing the Employment Relationship_ in this series.

3.6 Reputation

If the most important thing to you is to gain a reputation as a hard bargainer, or as someone who always gets what they want, you may be storing up trouble for the future. You can't always win, and if you are known as someone who takes a hard line, others will be far less willing to compromise, and conflicts are more likely to arise. Much better to aim for a reputation for fair dealing and problem solving.

3.7 Expectations about outcomes

Don't be too fixed about your desired outcome. If you have decided beforehand what this is going to be, you will be less inclined to be flexible when alternative solutions appear. And, however confident you are of the strength of your argument, there is always a danger that some factor will emerge which you have not anticipated.

When it comes to formal negotiations, it is always good to know what your limits are, and to be flexible within them. You will learn more about this later on in this session.

3.8 Pressure of work and deadlines

Making decisions under pressure of a deadline can have advantages and disadvantages.

Activity 32   3 mins

Can you think of one advantage of a tight deadline in decision making and one disadvantage?

Advantage

_____

Disadvantage

_____

One advantage could be that, if you have prepared your case thoroughly, you may be able to push a decision through before the other side has had time to think out all the implications.

A disadvantage could be that decisions made under pressure may not satisfy either party in the long run. It is unlikely that all the factors will have been fully explored, so the optimum solution for both parties will not have been identified, and the other party may be left resentful and ready for revenge at a later date.

3.9 Location

The influence of location can be very strong for some people – whether it is the general layout of the office environment or, more specifically, the location in which discussions take place.

Some people may feel more confident on their home territory. They also have the advantage of immediate access to files, plans and other information which might be useful. On the other hand, they might gather a great deal of background information by going to the other party's offices, and be more able to control the point in the discussions at which the meeting comes to an end.

The layout of the meeting area can also be a strong influence on what happens during a discussion session.

Activity 33

Assuming that there are just two people involved, which of the following seating arrangements would provide the most constructive environment to carry out discussions? Put a circle round the one you think is best.

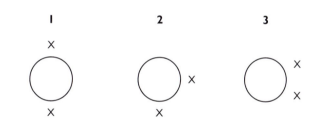

You should have chosen the second option. This gives the parties the best chance of building a rapport. Option I, where they sit opposite each other, tends to give a feeling of confrontation – as though battle lines have been drawn. In option 3 they are sitting next to each other. This may avoid the confrontation problem but their close proximity may be constricting and they will be unable to use body language, such as eye contact, to check each other's reactions and understanding.

3.10 Using influence to promote action

Activity 34 · 3 mins

In each of the following situations, identify the factors used to influence team members to carry out the decision in the way the manager wants. Use the list of influencing factors discussed in this session,

a Frances Dean commands the respect of her team members. They are convinced about her ability, and aim to be loyal. She uses this influence to encourage her staff to implement decisions.

_____

_____

b Marco Luciana recognizes that his team would be more able to implement decisions if he re-organized the office layout. This will bring certain team members closer together and improve communication between them.

_____

_____

c Daniel Patterson is very highly trained in logistics and this expertise is recognized by his team. As a result, team members listen carefully to his suggestions and explanations on how to carry out certain operations.

_____

_____

You should have recognized that:

■ method (a) involves the influence of personal relationships;
■ method (b) involves the influence of location;
■ method (c) involves the influence of expertise.

4 Persuading

Personal power is vital in all communication, whether it is formal or informal, to one person or to a thousand. Even if you have the best idea, the best strategy or the best product, you will get a much better result if you are able to get other people to 'buy in' to the idea. And getting people to buy in involves the skill of persuasion.

If you are going to persuade someone to do something you must first decide the following.

1 What objective you want to achieve.

2 What behaviour you want from the other person which will allow you to achieve your objective.

Once you are clear about these two things, you can concentrate on choosing the techniques that will persuade the other person to help you achieve your objective.

Persuasion techniques can be verbal or non-verbal.

4.1 Verbal persuasion techniques

The high street bookshops are full of books containing hints and tips on how to get ahead in business. Many of them describe weird and wonderful techniques that may work for the author, but would be totally inappropriate in your own workplace. One thing that they nearly all emphasize, however, is the importance of good verbal communication in getting what you want.

Verbal communication techniques fall into three groups:

- building rapport;
- boosting the other party's self-esteem;
- creating a positive atmosphere.

Building rapport

If you have a rapport with someone it means that you are on the same wave length as they are.

When building rapport, first impressions are all important. When you meet someone for the first time you pick up and give out all sorts of messages about each other without really noticing it. What you look like, the sound of your voice, mannerisms, and so on. This information is then processed internally and conclusions drawn as to whether you like or dislike the other person – and consequently whether you are going to get on with them or not.

Activity 35

5 mins

Imagine that a new recruit is due to join your team tomorrow morning. What verbal behaviour could you adopt to make her feel at ease – to build a rapport – as soon as she arrives? Try to think of four suggestions.

_____

_____

_____

_____

Your suggestions could have included:

- expressing pleasure at her arrival;
- chatting about everyday things that you both have in common (such as travelling to work);
- using her name frequently (when talking both to her and to other members of the team);
- asking a small favour of her – this will help her to feel valued;
- using appropriate humour to relax the situation;
- showing empathy, i.e. showing that you can understand how she is feeling.

You can also use a number of non-verbal techniques. These are discussed later on in this section.

EXTENSION I
You may like to read
*How to be Twice as
Smart* by Scott Witt. It
is one of many books
which give helpful ideas
on getting ahead in the
work place.

Boosting the other party's self-esteem

According to Scott Witt, one of the most effective ways of influencing people is to make them feel good about themselves. For example, you can simply ask someone to do something for you in such a way that they become anxious to do it because it makes them feel important.

You can boost someone's self-esteem by, for example:

- making them believe that they have a reputation to live up to;
- making them feel needed;
- asking questions that make them feel knowledgeable;
- making them feel that there is a challenge to be met.

Activity 36 · 3 mins

Next time you ask members of your workforce to do something, try saying something to boost their self-esteem first. Notice how much more enthusiastic they are about doing what you ask.

Creating a positive atmosphere

If you follow a few simple rules, you will find it is easy to create a positive atmosphere that encourages co-operation.

1 Use phrases such as 'We could …' or 'How would you feel if …' rather than 'You must …' or 'I can't …'. This will instil a feeling of collaboration rather than opposition in negotiations.

2 Make it clear that you are prepared to consider the other party's arguments constructively, and acknowledge that they have a valid viewpoint.

3 Give the other side the chance to talk without interrupting. You will learn much and avoid creating an atmosphere of dissent.

Neuro-linguistic programming

Neuro-linguistic programming (NLP) is a rather forbidding name for something quite straightforward. It is the term used for a study of the relationship between thinking, language and behaviour – **what** people do, **why** they do it and **how** they do it.

EXTENSION 3
A useful introduction to neuro-linguistic programming is given in *Introducing NLP* by Sue Knight.

Put very simply, by studying how people behave, you can tell what they are thinking. And, conversely, by behaving in a particular way you can influence how other people think. We have already seen how you can build rapport with another person by using eye contact, finding common topics of conversation and making them feel needed. In fact, most of us do this all the time without even realizing it. NLP takes the idea much further and can be an invaluable tool in developing relationships with other people in the organization.

4.2   Non-verbal persuasion techniques

The final skill you need in order to master the art of persuasion is the use of non-verbal communication.

Research shows that less than half of communication is through what you have to say. The rest is partly communicated through the way you look and partly through the way you act, and more tends to be conveyed by appearance than by action.

Clearly, then, appearance is a vital element in persuading people to behave in the way you want.

The diagram below shows how your appearance affects the way you see yourself, and how this, in turn, affects how others see you. If you look and act

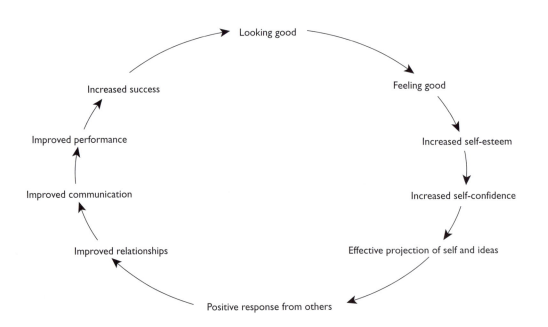

as though you are successful you will feel successful, if you feel successful then people will assume that you are successful, and so on.

You can communicate non-verbal messages about yourself in many ways. Some of the most important include using your:

- eyes;
- facial expression;
- voice;
- gestures;
- posture;
- appearance.

Eyes

EXTENSION 7
How to Communicate Effectively by Bert Decker is a highly readable guide to the use of body language and non-verbal communication.

In general, your eyes are the only part of you that directly connect with the person you are talking to. You can use your eyes to intimidate, build rapport, plead, show affection or fear. It largely depends on the length of time you maintain eye contact.

In one-to-one conversations, you should make eye contact for between five and ten seconds at a time. You may want to practise this with a friend, to get a sense of what it feels like.

Facial expression

You may think that you are a natural 'smiler', but research has shown that only about a third of people naturally smile most of the time, while a third are neutral and a third smile very little.

An open, smiling expression makes you appear friendly and, as the Book of Proverbs says: 'He who would have friends, let him show himself friendly'. It has also been claimed that smiling actually makes you feel more cheerful and positive.

You may find it helpful to ask other people which third of the 'smilers' you belong to. Then, if necessary, practise smiling more – even when you don't feel like it. You will find that it makes you feel better.

Voice

Your voice is a tool, which you can use to great effect if you know how. It conveys energy, emotion and mood. Research shows that, in situations where the other person can't see you (such as during a telephone conversation), your tone and intonation convey 84% of the message they receive.

Activity 37 · 5 mins

Next time you ring someone up and they respond by saying 'Hello', think about what clues their voice is giving out about their feelings, mood, confidence and attitude towards you. Then try to be aware of the messages you are sending through your own voice.

Gestures

Your gestures should reflect the energy you feel inside. Italians use their hands, arms and facial expressions to support what they are saying, and this not only reinforces their verbal message, but it keeps the listener's attention and introduces an emotional factor which makes what they say far more arresting. Arms flung wide and eyes cast to heaven cannot fail to attract the listener's attention.

On the other hand, physical habits such as rocking from one foot to the other, rattling money in your pockets or scratching your head can be very distracting and should be avoided.

Activity 38 · 3 mins

Ask your friends to tell you if you have any physical mannerism that you are not aware of. Then try to notice every time you do it so that, gradually, you can stop doing it altogether.

Posture

Everyone has their own style of posture and movement, but some give out messages that you would rather not send. Standing in a slumped position is very negative and often implies low self-esteem. It also suggests that you are uninterested and lacking in energy – not a good idea if you want to give an air of self-confidence. Let's face it, you never see a politician or celebrity slumping!

The best position is to stand upright with your weight slightly forward and balanced equally on both feet. Avoid crossing your arms or legs, as these can appear as a defensive barrier against other people.

Appearance

Whatever the way you dress, it should be appropriate for the environment in which you work. Your appearance says a lot about how you feel about yourself.

It reflects your general attitude so, if you dress sloppily, others will perceive you as a sloppy manager. If you dress smartly the impression you give will be far more dynamic and positive. The same principle applies whether the organization dress code is formal or casual.

Think about your normal appearance at work. What impression do you give? Are you always well groomed, with well-pressed clothes and well-cut hair? Do you dress in that particular style because you always have done, or because you know it suits you? Are the colours you wear the right ones for you? Are some of you clothes really past their wear-by date?

You could ask other people to honestly give an opinion about your appearance. Consider having a colour analysis session. It can be very helpful in identifying colours and styles that really do you justice.

5 Negotiating

King Solomon was faced with a problem. Two women had come to him seeking justice, both claiming that they were the mother of the same baby boy. How did Solomon solve the problem? Well, he pronounced that the only fair thing to do was to divide the baby in half and give one half to each woman. Faced with the prospect of the death of her child, the real mother renounced her rights. Solomon deduced from this that she was the true mother.

King Solomon was a past master at resolving conflict through negotiation. He listened to both arguments, identified the facts, and found a solution that was fair to both sides.

This section looks at negotiation – the skill of finding a solution to conflicting needs and wants which, while not always giving either party everything they want, at least usually provides them with enough to feel that they have received what is fair.

Negotiating is only necessary when you don't have enough positional power to get what you want by simply issuing an instruction.

5.1 The nature of negotiation

Louise asks one of her team, Nico, to take part in a market research project that will involve him in about 10 hours' work a week for seven weeks. Nico is interested, but points out that being on the project will mean 10 hours a week less in which to do his normal job.

Louise expects this. Her response is to offer Nico some extra clerical help, but Nico feels that this will still leave him about five hours a week short.

Louise suggests that Nico can probably cope with this. Nico is reluctant.

Louise points out that being on the market research project will be a useful career move for Nico. Nico agrees and thanks Louise for the opportunity but says that he is still concerned about the additional pressure and the possibility of his normal work falling behind.

The two colleagues consider several options.

Louise finally bridges the gap by agreeing to transfer one of Nico's routine tasks to another colleague, Grace, for the duration of the project, on condition that Nico spends a reasonable amount of time training and briefing Grace in how to do it.

This kind of 'dealing', which goes on a lot at work, is a classic example of negotiation.

All negotiations have five main characteristics.

- There is a gap to be bridged between two (and sometimes more) positions.
- Both sides recognize that it is desirable to reach an agreement.
- Both sides are willing to make concessions in order to reach agreement.
- Neither side knows in advance how much the other is willing to concede.
- The negotiation process consists of repeated exchanges of messages.

Both sides in a negotiation should set themselves SMART objectives.

Specific
Measurable
Achievable
Relevant
Time bound

The outcome of negotiations should be a decision which is, in the circumstances, satisfactory to both sides.

Usually this means a compromise of some kind. Typically, each side enters the negotiations recognizing that they may not get everything they want. On the other hand, each will have a limit beyond which they are not willing to go.

Negotiations may be formal or informal.

5.2 Formal negotiation

Some of the negotiations you may become involved in at work may be formal, for example when:

- discussing changes to pay and conditions with union or staff association representatives;
- seeking an agreement with suppliers or customers over contract terms or compensation for poor work;
- agreeing the terms for a collaborative venture.

Often such negotiations will be carried out in accordance with formal guidelines and with specified personnel involved. They may even involve an external body which is highly skilled in such negotiations, such as the Advisory, Conciliation and Arbitration Service (ACAS) or a trade union.

Activity 39 · 5 mins

Make a note of any formal negotiations that you or your colleagues have recently been involved in at work. Who took part? Were they conducted according to formal guidelines? Was any external body involved? Did each side feel satisfied with the outcome?

_____

_____

_____

_____

_____

5.3 Informal negotiation

Most of the time the negotiations you become involved in will be informal rather than formal.

A great deal of your time as a first line manager will be taken up in negotiating with your team in regard to such matters as:

■ workload;
■ time off;
■ working conditions;
■ co-operative projects.

Whether the negotiations are formal or informal, the same basic process applies.

5.4 Six stages of negotiation

The size and complexity of negotiations can vary enormously: from international conferences of global significance at one extreme to planning a staff outing at the other. But whatever their size, all negotiations will go through the same six stages.

■ Preparation.
■ Exchanging initial views.
■ Exploring possible solutions.
■ Identifying common ground.
■ Reaching a compromise.
■ Implementing the compromise.

While we look briefly at each one in turn, check back to the case study of Louise and Nico to see how it works in practice.

Step		Action
1	Prepare	■ Know your stuff. Don't get caught out by unexpected revelations from the other side. ■ Decide your objectives – what is the least you will settle for? ■ What will your strategy be?
2	Exchange initial views	■ Give a brief statement of your starting position. ■ Find out about the other side by getting them to talk about their concerns, motives and aims. Try to identify their strengths and weaknesses. ■ Clarify the size of the gap between you.
3	Explore possible solutions	■ Consider all possible compromises without committing either side. ■ Point out the benefits of finding a mutually satisfactory solution. ■ Encourage the other person to make constructive suggestions. ■ Find out what the other side values that it costs you little to give.
4	Identify common ground	■ Find out what you both agree on and then build on it.
5	Reach a compromise	■ Use your skills of persuasion to encourage the other side to reach a compromise. ■ If necessary, give a small concession to avoid them losing face.
6	Implement the compromise	■ Write down and confirm the details of what has been agreed. ■ Agree a timetable for implementation. ■ If the compromise is complicated, agree a detailed plan which includes: actions to be taken, deadlines, who will be involved, who will be informed, how the plan will be monitored and evaluated.

5.5 Negotiating skills

In Session B you learned about certain behaviours which would build an atmosphere of trust and co-operation in your team, but there are other behaviours that are particularly useful in negotiating. They are as follows.

Concentrate on the reasons behind the other side's stance rather than the stance itself

If, say, a team member asks for more pay, look at the whole picture rather than just the pay demand itself. For instance, if you discover that the additional money is needed because of child care problems, it may be that other factors can be brought into the negotiations in order to find a solution, such as holiday allowances or flexitime.

Attack the problem rather than the person

Don't get involved in a spiral of personal attacks. That does no good to anyone, and takes the focus away from the problem itself.

Move the discussion forward rather than getting trapped in counter-arguments

There is no benefit in simply disagreeing with the other side's position. You should aim to look for ways of finding an area of common ground, then move forward from there.

State your reasons first, then disagree

The phrase 'No, I disagree' is like a brick wall. It brings the other party to a full stop without offering any way forward. Much better to give your reasons for disagreeing first, then say that you disagree. You could say, for example, 'While you say that the yarn is stripey because of our poor spinning, it could be that your tufting machine is not working properly. So I can't agree…'.

Never exaggerate

We have already learned that behaviour breeds behaviour. So, if you exaggerate the facts, the other side will too. Once you have lost sight of the real facts, you cannot negotiate a lasting solution.

Remember the value of openness

In Session B we learned that if you are open in the way you communicate, the other side is much more likely to be objective in the negotiations.

Use questions as a negotiating tool

Never assume that you know all there is to know about the other side's position. Ask questions to discover their motives, beliefs, prejudices, and bargaining strengths and weaknesses. By asking questions you move the focus away from your own position, and may discover new areas of agreement which could move the negotiations forward.

Keep checking

Make sure that you summarize the position at regular intervals so that both sides know exactly where they are. Any progress you make thereafter will be based on a solid foundation.

It is important to remember that successful negotiations depend on both sides paying very careful attention to what the other side is saying. In order to get a precise understanding, they need to ask each other many kinds of question, such as those that follow.

- Reflecting   'So what you're saying is…'
- Supporting   'Yes, that's a very positive suggestion. So can we…?'
- Disagreeing   'Won't that cost too much?'
- Constructing   'Would it help if…?'
- Clarifying   'Isn't the point that…?'
- Interpreting   'Are you suggesting…?'
- Confirming   'So we agree that…'
- Testing   'Would it be right to say that…?'

Activity 40

5 mins

Make a note of the eight behaviours listed above. Next time you are involved in negotiations with someone, either at work or at home, use the list as a memory jogger of the behaviours you should be adopting. Then make a brief note of those which worked well and those in which you need more practice.

Randolph Provisions are negotiating the price on the purchase of corned beef from a new supplier. Their buyer is prepared to pay a maximum of £0.39 per tin for 22,000 packs of 24 tins, but her objective is to get the price down to £0.35. The supplier's salesman is prepared to accept a minimum of £0.37, but is aiming to achieve £0.41. However, he will accept a slightly lower price if the order quantity is higher.

Activity 41

3 mins

The two negotiators can reach agreement across a range of prices.

What is the maximum price in this range?

_____

What is the minimum price in this range?

_____

The range within which the agreed price will fall is the area where the buyer's and the supplier's maximum and minimum prices overlap. We can show this negotiable area in a table below, with a dash indicating a price that one or other side is not prepared to consider.

Buyer's range	35	36	37	38	39	–	–
Supplier's range	–	–	37	38	39	40	41

The price range is therefore between 37 pence and 39 pence, but remember that neither side actually knows where the other's maximum and minimum lie.

It is up to the two negotiators to use their skills to try to persuade each other in the direction of the most favourable outcome for themselves. Above 39 pence and below 37 pence, agreement is, of course, not possible.

Activity 42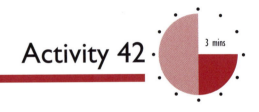

3 mins

What would happen if there were a stalemate, for example if the buyer refused to go above £0.36?

_____

_____

_____

The supplier might agree to shift his minimum price downwards if:

- the buyer increased the order quantity;
- the buyer agreed to a long-term contract;
- the buyer agreed to take some other product from the supplier as well.

Self-assessment 3 · 12 mins

1 State whether each of the following is a command, a request or a plea.

a 'Prepare this order for Mentrim Ltd, would you?' _____

b 'Don't argue, just do it!' _____

c 'Please do your best to get this done on time. It's for the good of the whole team, you know!' _____

d 'Can you just adjust this so that the legs don't protrude? Thanks.' _____

2 Which one of the following is the best advice to a first line manager when team members haven't carried out a task they have been asked to do?

a Ask someone else to do the job.

b Ask the team members whether your instructions were clear.

c Initiate immediate disciplinary action.

d Reconsider your decision and look at alternatives.

3 Suggest two situations when expert knowledge might be particularly valuable.

a _____

b _____

4 Suggest three ways in which you can boost someone's self-esteem.

a _____

b _____

c _____

5 You can use neuro-linguistic programming to build a _____ with someone.

6   Suggest six ways in which you can use non-verbal communication to influence someone's behaviour towards you.

_____

_____

_____

_____

_____

_____

7   If one side clearly loses in negotiations, what two risks are being run?

a _____

b _____

8   What are the six steps in negotiation?

1 _____

2 _____

3 _____

4 _____

5 _____

6 _____

Answers to these questions can be found on pages 88–9.

6 Summary

- There are four ways of achieving what you want at work.

  - Instructing – where you have sufficient power and authority to **tell** someone what to do.
  - Influencing – where you bring the whole context of the situation to bear on the other person, including the quality of your past and current working relationship, his or her wants, needs and fears.
  - Persuading – where you use all your verbal and non-verbal skills to get the other person to agree.
  - Negotiating – where you each have the same bargaining power, and each has to compromise in order to get something of what you want.

- Requests are generally the most suitable way of making your requirements known. They should:

  - be polite and personal;
  - leave time for questions and a reply.

- The main factors of influence are:

  - personal relationships;
  - position power;
  - formality;
  - knowledge and expertise;
  - gender, race and age;
  - reputation;
  - expectations about outcomes;
  - pressure of work and deadlines;
  - location.

- If you are going to persuade someone you must first decide:

  - what objective you want to achieve;
  - what behaviour you want from that other person which will allow you to achieve your objective.

- Verbal influencing techniques include:

  - building rapport;
  - boosting the other party's self-esteem;
  - creating a constructive environment.

- Neuro-linguistic programming (NLP) is a study of the relationship between thinking, language and behaviour – **what** people do, **why** they do it and **how** they do it.

■ Non-verbal influencing techniques include communicating with your:

   ■ eyes;
   ■ facial expression;
   ■ voice;
   ■ gestures;
   ■ posture;
   ■ appearance.

■ Negotiations are a specialized kind of meeting. They depend heavily on clear communication and accurate understanding. Negotiators typically question each other closely, and repeat and summarize ideas in order to ensure that they have not misunderstood one another.

■ The agreements reached during negotiations need to be recorded with care.

■ The six stages of negotiation are:

   ■ preparation;
   ■ exchange of initial views;
   ■ exploring possible solutions;
   ■ identifying common ground;
   ■ reaching a compromise;
   ■ implementing the compromise.

Performance checks

▮ 1 Quick quiz

Question 1   What is the process through which the brain interprets information received from the senses?

_____

Question 2   '_____' is the sense that enables us to 'feel' what people are like.

Question 3   Fill in the empty boxes.

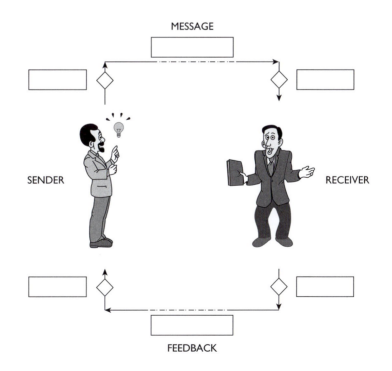

Question 4   What three pieces of information does feedback give the original sender of a message?

_____

_____

_____

Question 5   What are 'of course', 'naturally', 'by the way' and 'I can't because…' examples of?

_____

_____

Question 6   What do the letters SWOT stand for?

_____

_____

_____

_____

Question 7   Suggest three strategies you could use in forming an external network.

_____

_____

_____

Question 8   A _____ _____ is a ready-reference list of people who are willing and able to give you the information you need when you need it.

Question 9   A _____ _____ _____ is a group of people who enjoy sharing knowledge and enthusiasm for a particular topic.

Question 10   Research shows that 7% of communication is through what you have to_____. Of the other 93%, 55% is communicated through the way you _____ and 38% through the way you _____.

Question 11   In negotiations, what do we mean by the 'negotiable area'?

_____

_____

Question 12   The chances of achieving success in negotiations are greatly improved if each side honestly communicates their _____ and _____.

Question 13   Give two reasons why it is not a good idea for one side to win a dispute outright and the other to lose.

_____

_____

Answers to these questions can be found on pages 90–1.

60 mins

2 Workbook assessment

Jack Taylor has recently been appointed manager of a team of ten in a large firm of travel agents. The team comprises eight holiday bookings staff, one administrative assistant and one technical assistant responsible for maintenance of the computer system.

Until his appointment, Jack worked for 15 years as a holiday bookings assistant at another location within the company. Sarah Price, an experienced member of his new team, had expected to be appointed and is very resentful of Jack's appointment. She feels that she has more local knowledge than Jack and gets on well with most of the team.

Jack arranges a meeting with Sarah soon after he arrives to resolve the differences he feels exist between them. He has heard about a new opportunity coming up soon that he thinks might be attractive to Sarah, and hopes to persuade her to apply.

When Sarah arrives she sits very straight in her chair with her arms folded tightly and looks directly at Jack, making him feel quite uncomfortable. He tries to make her relax by chatting about general issues, but she will barely answer his questions and says very little.

_____

Write down your answers to the following questions

■   What does Sarah's behaviour suggest about her attitudes and feelings?
■   What can Jack do to try to improve their relationship?
■   How might Jack go about persuading Sarah to apply for the new opportunity?

Reflect and review

1 Reflect and review

Now that you have completed your work on *Influencing Others at Work*, let's review the workbook objectives. The first objective was:

■ use your senses to gather information from those around you.

Communication is a two-way process: we send messages out and we receive feedback in return. But many messages have hidden (or covert) meanings which we need to be able to pick up. This is done through the five physical senses together with the sixth sense, intuition. But messages can be distorted by mind filters and interference.

Things to think about include:

■ What filters do you and the other members of your team use that might get in the way of clear communication?

_____

_____

_____

■ How can you ensure that the messages you send and receive are not distorted by interference?

_____

_____

_____

■ How can you help your team to communicate more clearly?

_____
_____
_____

The next objective was:

■ use the technique of whole body listening to pick up hidden messages.

Whole body listening enables us to concentrate thoroughly on the messages being communicated to us. We can tell a lot about what someone really means by noting the way they speak, the types of words they use, and their body language.

You could think about the following questions:

■ What are the hidden messages that you receive every day but which, up to now, you have not identified?

_____
_____
_____

■ What hidden messages do you give out when communicating with your team which reduce the impact of what you are trying to say?

_____
_____
_____

■ What steps can you take to develop the skill of whole body listening – for both you and your team?

_____
_____
_____

The next objective was:

■ explain the value of networking, and create a network to promote both your work objectives and social interests.

Networking puts at your disposal a huge reservoir of knowledge and experience which you otherwise would not have. In a knowledge network the people in it are normally unaware of the fact that they are providing information purely in order for you to achieve your set objectives. They are happy to provide information because it makes them feel valued.

Mutual interest networks exist for the benefit of all the members. Everyone contributes knowledge and expertise for the benefit of everyone else in the network.

The success of all networking depends on your skill at building rapport.

Think about:

- What personal objective do you have which could be helped by developing a knowledge network?

  _____

  _____

  _____

- What networks do you already have at work which could provide you with useful information?

  _____

  _____

  _____

- What steps will you take to build rapport with the people around you?

  _____

  _____

  _____

The last objective was:

- to be able to apply the principles of influence and persuasion to achieve objectives.

There are a number of factors of influence which will affect one or other side in a negotiation and you can use these to strengthen your bargaining position. You should also recognize those factors that might influence you in a negotiating situation. Means of persuasion include verbal and non-verbal techniques.

Points to think about include the following.

■ Which factors of influence can I use to advantage when dealing with my staff or with other people inside and outside the organization?

_____

_____

_____

■ What strategies can I adopt to improve my powers of persuasion?

_____

_____

_____

2 Action plan

Use this plan to further develop for yourself a course of action you want to take. Make a note in the left-hand column of the issues or problems you want to tackle, and then decide what you intend to do, and make a note in Column 2.

The resources you need might include time, materials, information or money. You may need to negotiate for some of them, but they could be something easily acquired, like half an hour of somebody's time, or a chapter of a book. Put whatever you need in Column 3. No plan means anything without a timescale, so put a realistic target completion date in Column 4.

Finally, describe the outcome you want to achieve as a result of this plan, whether it is for your own benefit or advancement, or a more efficient way of doing things.

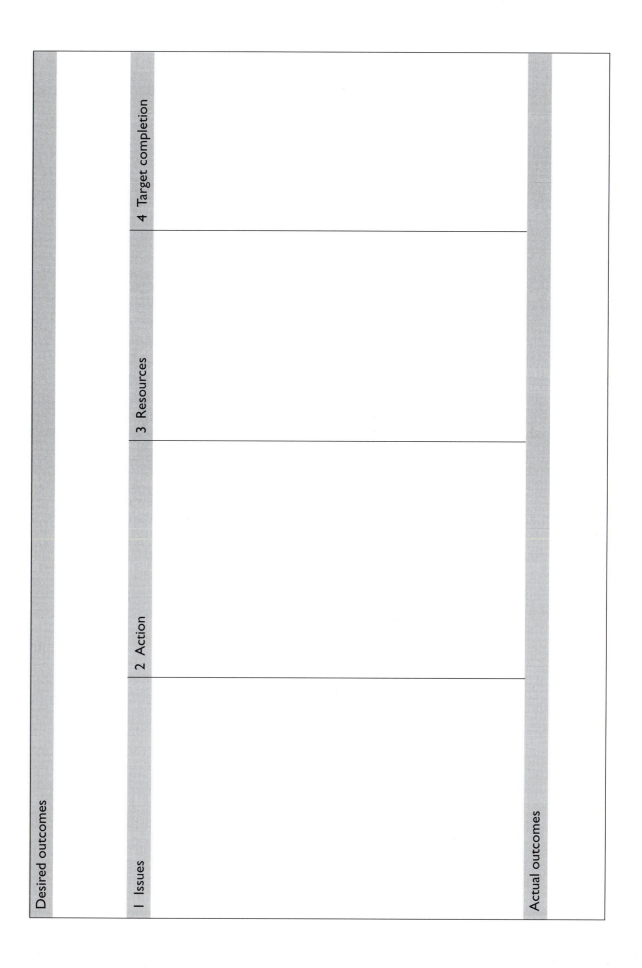

Desired outcomes

1 Issues	2 Action	3 Resources	4 Target completion

Actual outcomes

3 Extensions

Extension I	Book	*How to be Twice as Smart*
	Author	Scott Witt
	Edition	1983
	Publisher	Reward Books

Extension 2	Book	*How to Win Friends and Influence People*
	Author	Dale Carnegie
	Edition	1984
	Publisher	Chancellor Press

Extension 3	Book	*NLP at Work*
	Author	Sue Knight
	Edition	2002
	Publisher	Nicholas Brealey Publishing

Extension 4	Book	*Body Talk – the skills of positive image*
	Author	Judi James
	Edition	1995
	Publisher	Spiro Press

Extension 5	Book	*Networking for Success*
	Author	Carol Harris
	Edition	2000
	Publisher	Oak Tree Press

Extension 6	Book	*Negotiating Persuading and Influencing*
	Author	Alan Fowler
	Edition	2000
	Publisher	CIPD

Extension 7	Book	*How to communicate effectively*
	Author	Bert Decker
	Edition	1990
	Publisher	Kogan Page

These extensions can be taken up via your ILM Centre. They will either have them or will arrange that you have access to them.

4 Answers to self-assessment questions

1 We use our **SENSES** to build an image of what the people around us are like and how they will effect us.

2 Our five physical senses are sight, smell, hearing, taste and touch.

3 The communication process consists of a sender sending a **MESSAGE** to a receiver, and in return receiving **FEEDBACK**.

4 Feedback is of vital importance in the communication process because it tells the sender whether (a) the message has been understood, and (b) whether the desired outcome has been achieved.

5 Three techniques which will help you to ignore distractions when someone is speaking are:

- taking notes;
- playing mind games;
- using memory techniques.

6 The secret of active listening is to show that you are truly interested.

7

Type of listener	Their attention is internal	They are listening with their whole body
They think their own thoughts, make evaluations and judgements. They worry and concentrate on what just happened, what was just said or even what might happen next.	✓	
Their gaze is on the other person.		✓
They are in a state of curiosity. Their attention is entirely on the other person.		✓
Their language is likely to be 'I', 'me' centred.	✓	

8 You can judge the level of knowledge and language ability of someone about whom you know virtually nothing by:

- asking them;
- observing their body language.

9 A speaker's body language can:
a reduce the speaker's credibility by being distracting;
b weaken the message if it conflicts with it.

Self-assessment 2 on page 44

1 Networking can be defined as the creation and use of personal contacts for one's own **BENEFIT** or for the **BENEFIT** of a group.

2 In a network you use your contacts with other people to help both you and them to become more successful. A social group doesn't necessarily have any specific aim.

3 Networks can be classified as internal/external or knowledge networks/mutual interest networks.

4 You could develop an internal network by:

- establishing regular email correspondence with someone who has knowledge that will help you;
- joining committees;
- joining a company sports team.

5 A network designed specifically to benefit all members equally is a mutual interest network (MIN).

6 You should never ask advice from someone who usually charges for such information.

7 SWOT stands for strengths, weaknesses, opportunities and threats.

8 Yes. So long as you are on the same wavelength, it doesn't matter if you don't share their opinions.

Self-assessment 3 on page 73

1 The correct answers are as follows.

a 'Prepare this order for Mentrim Ltd, would you?'	REQUEST
b 'Don't argue, just do it!'	ORDER
c 'Please do your best to get this done on time. It's for the good of the whole team, you know!'	PLEA
d 'Can you just adjust this so that the legs don't protrude? Thanks.'	REQUEST

2 The best advice is (b), when you would try to find out whether your instructions were clear. A simple misunderstanding might be the reason why the team members haven't carried out the task.

3   Expert knowledge is particularly valuable if you are suffering under the negative influences of weak position power or poor personal relationships.

4   You can boost someone's self-esteem by:

- making them believe that they have a reputation to live up to
- making them feel needed
- asking questions that make them feel knowledgeable
- making them feel that there is a challenge to be met.

5   You can use neuro-linguistic programming to build a **RAPPORT** with someone.

6   Suggest six means through which you can use non-verbal communication are through your eyes, facial expression, voice, gestures, posture and appearance.

7   If one side clearly loses in a negotiation, the risks are that:
- someone more senior on the other side may repudiate the agreement
- the losing negotiator may feel resentful and seek revenge at a later date.

8   The six steps in negotiation are:

1   preparation
2   exchange of initial views
3   exploring possible solutions
4   identifying common ground
5   reaching a compromise
6   implementing the compromise.

5 Answers to activities

Your answer should have been as follows.

**Activity 4
on page 7**

2   Paul has 'mismatch', 'internal', 'future' and 'towards' filters.

3   Jan has 'past', 'away from', 'match' and 'external' filters.

**Activity 12
on page 19**

Signals common in the UK that you might have listed include:

- shaking the head to show disagreement;
- beckoning with the hands;
- waving to attract attention;
- waving both hands from side to side to indicate 'stop';
- pointing;
- clapping;
- shrugging the shoulders to indicate 'don't know' or 'don't care';
- raising the arms to surrender;
- shaking a fist to show anger.

6 Answers to the quick quiz

Answer 1   The process through which the brain interprets information received from the senses is called 'perception'.

Answer 2   **'INTUITION'** is the sense that enables us to 'feel' what people are like.

Answer 3

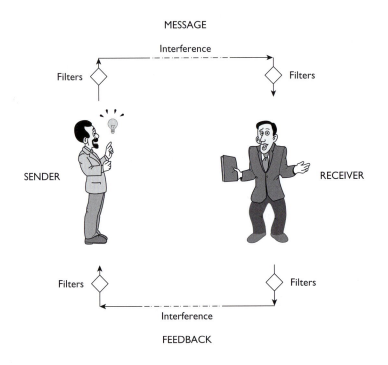

Answer 4   Feedback tells the original sender whether:

- the message has got through;
- action, if any, has been or will be taken;
- the purpose has been achieved.

Answer 5   They are all 'flag' words that indicate that the speaker doesn't mean what he or she says.

Answer 6   Strengths, Weaknesses, Opportunities and Threats.

Answer 7   Three strategies you could use in forming an external network are:

- joining a special interest club;
- using internet chat rooms;
- developing social links with people in other organizations.

Answer 8   A **KNOWLEDGE NETWORK** is a ready-reference list of people who are willing and able to give you the information you need when you need it.

Answer 9   A **MUTUAL INTEREST NETWORK** is a group of people who enjoy sharing knowledge and enthusiasm for a particular topic.

Answer 10   Research shows that 7% of communication is through what you have to **SAY**. Of the other 93%, 55% is communicated through the way you **LOOK** and 38% through the way you **ACT**.

Answer 11   In negotiations, the 'negotiable area' is the area where the maximum and minimum positions of the two sides overlap, and where agreement will eventually be reached.

Answer 12   The chances of success are greatly improved if each side honestly communicates their **THOUGHTS** and **FEELINGS**.

Answer 13   It is not a good idea for one side to win a dispute outright and the other to lose because:

- if one side has clearly lost the agreement it may be repudiated by more senior people on that side
- a losing negotiator may feel resentful, and may seek revenge at some later date.

7 Certificate

Completion of this certificate by an authorized person shows that you have worked through all the parts of this workbook and satisfactorily completed the assessments. The certificate provides a record of what you have done that may be used for exemptions or as evidence of prior learning against other nationally certificated qualifications.

superseries

Influencing Others at Work

....

has satisfactorily completed this workbook

Name of signatory ....

Position ....

Signature ....

Date ....

Official stamp

Pergamon
Flexible
Learning

Fifth Edition

superseries

FIFTH EDITION

Workbooks in the series:

For prices and availability please telephone our order helpline
or email

+44 (0) 1865 474010
directorders@elsevier.com

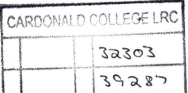